D1479886

Sight-Singing

For SSA

A Practical Sight-Singing Course For Beginning And Intermediate Choirs

By Joyce Eilers and Emily Crocker

HAL•LEONARD®

7777 W. BLUEMOUND RD. P.O. BOX 13819 MILWAUKEE, WI 53213

TABLE OF CONTENTS

How To Use This Book

Sight-Singing For SSA can be a practical and effective program for treble choirs from middle school or junior high through adult. Specific suggestions and step-by-step lesson plans are included in the Teacher's Manual (Hal Leonard #47819106). Briefly, sight-singing success is dependent upon a few basic principles:

- Singers are intelligent and willing. They can and will learn to sight-read quickly and well.
- Rhythm accounts for more than 50% of the difficulty in sight-singing. Always emphasize and reinforce rhythmic comprehension. Go beyond understanding to habit.
- Limit the time for sight-reading. 10-15 minutes a day should be sufficient.
- Remember the value of repetition. Go back and review previously-covered material for extra reinforcement and confidence-building.
- Everyone should be involved at all times, either by studying or practicing your own part, or by singing each other's part.
- Always be musical, whether working with songs or exercises.
- Transfer your sight-singing skills to learning music for concert performance. Constantly fine-tune your skills.

Introduction

Notes On The Staff

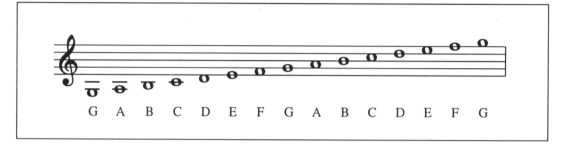

Notes On The Keyboard

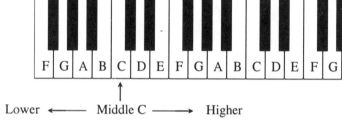

Lower ←——— Middle C ———→ Higher

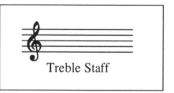

Treble Staff

Higher voices usually sing notes on the treble staff (above middle C).

DO NOT PHOTOCOPY

Rhythm – Let's Begin

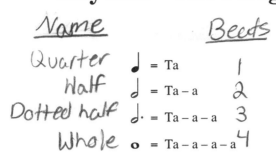

Name		Beats
Quarter	♩ = Ta	1
Half	♩ = Ta – a	2
Dotted half	♩. = Ta – a – a	3
Whole	o = Ta – a – a – a	4

Count each line.

① 𝄴 ♩ ♩ ♩ ♩ | ♩ ♩ ♩ ♩ | ♩ ♩ ♩ ♩ | ♩ ♩ ♩ ♩

② ♩ ♩ | ♩ ♩ | ♩ ♩ | ♩ ♩

③ ♩. ♩ | ♩. ♩ | ♩. ♩ | ♩. ♩

④ o | o | o | o

Count each line separately and in any combination.

⑤ 𝄴 ♩ ♩ ♩ | ♩ ♩ ♩ | ♩ ♩ ♩ | o

⑥ ♩ ♩ ♩ ♩ | ♩. ♩ | ♩ ♩ | o

⑦ ♩. ♩ | ♩ ♩ ♩ | ♩. ♩ | ♩ ♩

⑧ *♩ ♩ ♩ | ♩. ♩ | ♩ ♩ ♩ ♩ | o

*Stems may go up or down without affecting note value.

6

Adding Pitch To Rhythm

Example 1

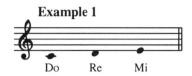

Do   Re   Mi

Sing each line separately and in any combination.

①

②

③

Example 2

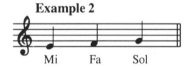

Mi   Fa   Sol

Sing each line separately and in any combination.

④

⑤

⑥

Five Note Exercises

Example

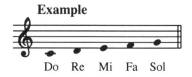

Do   Re   Mi   Fa   Sol

Sing each line separately and in any combination.

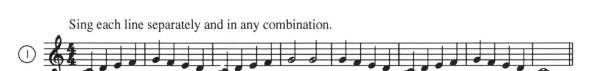

Travel On

Words and Music by
JOYCE EILERS and EMILY CROCKER

Fol - low the road, a - way, far a - way.

I must trav - el on, trav - el on.

Fair is the sum - mer, fair is the day.

Fol - low the road where it leads me.

Fair is the sum - mer, fair is the day.

Fol - low the road where it leads a - way.

rit.

Rests – Silent Beats

𝄽 = think ta

▬ = think ta – a

▬· = think ta – a – a

▬ = think ta – a – a – a

Count each line.

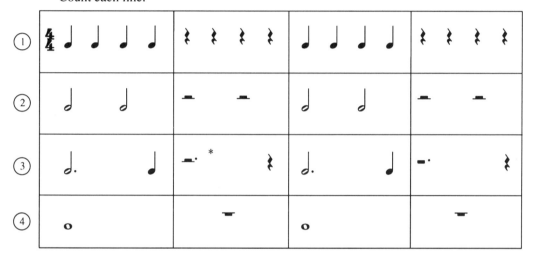

Count each line separately and in any combination.

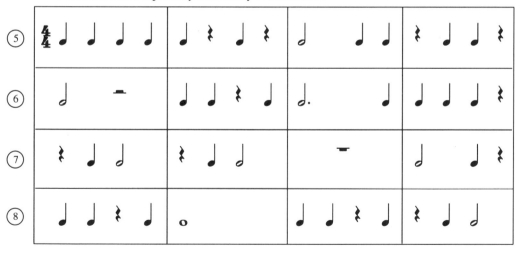

* Usually written ▭ ▬ 𝄽 ▭ or ▭ 𝄽 ▬ ▭

Pitch, Rhythm And Rests

Sing each line separately and in any combination.

Three Parts Together

Sing each line separately and in any combination.

Sing It Again

The exercises below are the same as those above, only with three parts connected by a bracket. Can you follow your own part until it stops at the double bar?

Singing Around

Sing each exercise separately and in any combination.

Sounds the Same, Looks Different

Good Night!

Traditional Rhyme

Music by **JOYCE EILERS**
and **EMILY CROCKER**

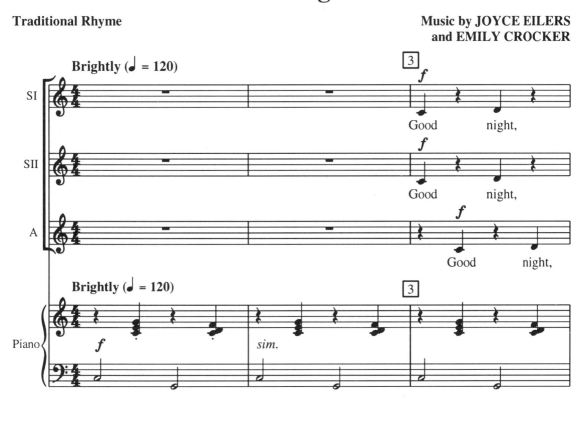

The Pitch Ladder
(Tonic Chord)

The notes "do," "mi," and "sol," when sung simultaneously or consecutively produce the tonic chord. Since most songs start on these notes, you can use them as a "pitch ladder" to help you find your starting pitch.

Finding The Starting Pitch

"Do" is the home tone of any major scale. After you find "do," use the pitch ladder (tonic chord) to establish tonality, then climb the pitch ladder to the starting pitch of the song.

Example

Do   Mi   Sol   Do   Sol   Mi   Do

Sing each line separately and in any combination.

①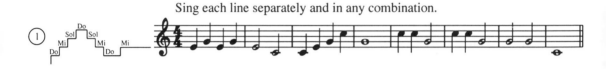

②

③

④

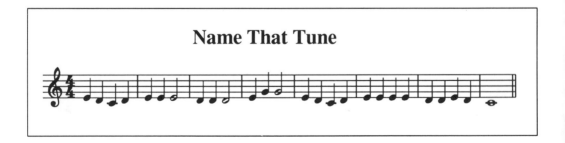

Name That Tune

The Full Scale

Example
Practice the complete scale, especially in reverse.

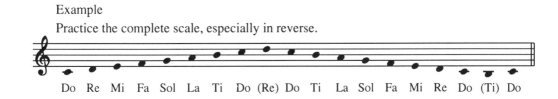

Do Re Mi Fa Sol La Ti Do (Re) Do Ti La Sol Fa Mi Re Do (Ti) Do

Use the pitch ladder to locate your starting pitch. Sing separately and in any combination.

①

②

③

④

⑤

⑥

Full Scale Exercises

For both exercises on this page, find the starting pitch with the pitch ladder.

Young Man Came A-Courting

Traditional Text

Music by **JOYCE EILERS**
and **EMILY CROCKER**

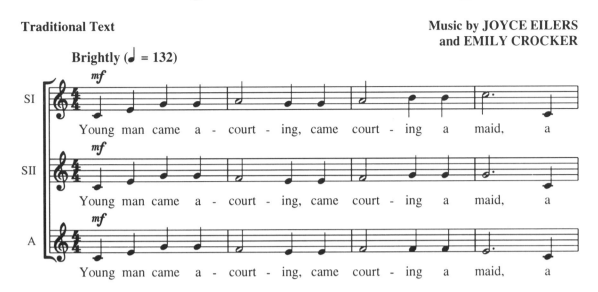

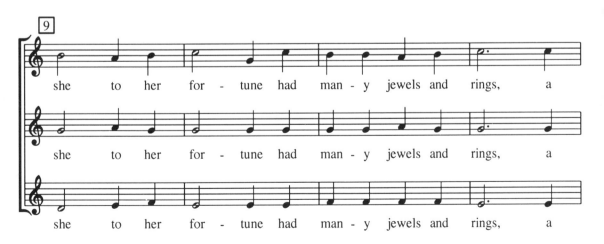

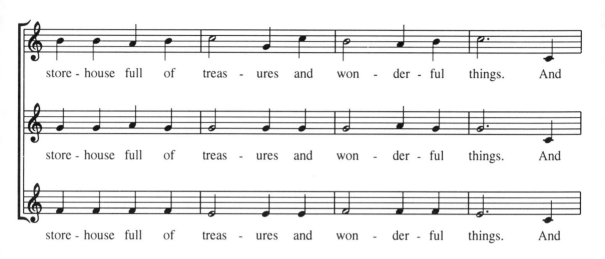

store - house full of treas - ures and won - der - ful things. And

store - house full of treas - ures and won - der - ful things. And

store - house full of treas - ures and won - der - ful things. And

17

so the day was named and the peo - ple all were there. The

so the day was named and the peo - ple all were there. The

so the day was named and the peo - ple all were there. The

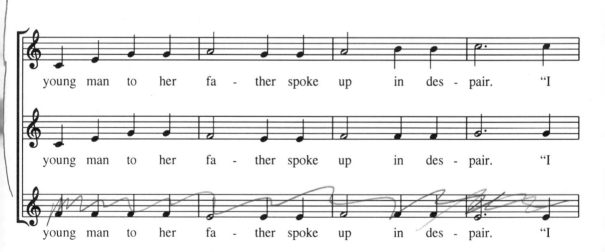

young man to her fa - ther spoke up in des - pair. "I

young man to her fa - ther spoke up in des - pair. "I

young man to her fa - ther spoke up in des - pair. "I

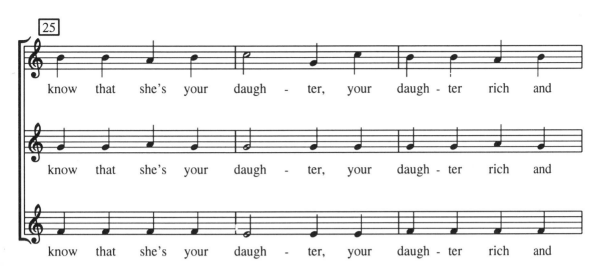

know that she's your daugh - ter, your daugh - ter rich and

know that she's your daugh - ter, your daugh - ter rich and

know that she's your daugh - ter, your daugh - ter rich and

fair. But all I real - ly want - ed was to

fair. But all I real - ly want - ed was to

fair. But all I real - ly want - ed was to

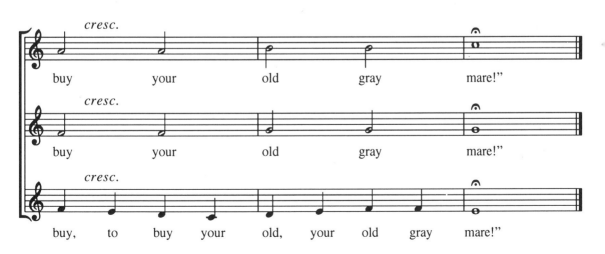

cresc.
buy your old gray mare!"

cresc.
buy your old gray mare!"

cresc.
buy, to buy your old, your old gray mare!"

SIGHT–SINGING FOR SSA — Singer's Edition

F – A New Key

If "do" is moved to a different line or space, all the other notes are changed as well. Drill until the examples are easy.

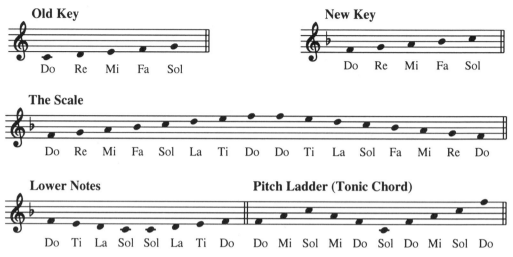

Old Key

Do Re Mi Fa Sol

New Key

Do Re Mi Fa Sol

The Scale

Do Re Mi Fa Sol La Ti Do Do Ti La Sol Fa Mi Re Do

Lower Notes

Do Ti La Sol Sol La Ti Do

Pitch Ladder (Tonic Chord)

Do Mi Sol Mi Do Sol Do Mi Sol Do

Sing separately, or in any combination.

Do these exercises sound familiar?

Warm-ups And Tune-ups
(Key of F)

Practice these broken chords often, until the patterns become habit. Always listen to pitch, tuning the last note of the chord to the first note.

do mi sol mi do sol do   do fa la fa do la do

ti re fa re ti sol ti   do mi sol do sol mi do

⑤ Almost there! Listen! Think!

sol do mi do sol   la do fa do la

ti re sol re ti   (etc.)

⑨ Now in reverse! You're on your own!

Chord Drills

Practice these chord drills, listening for balance, tuning and blend.

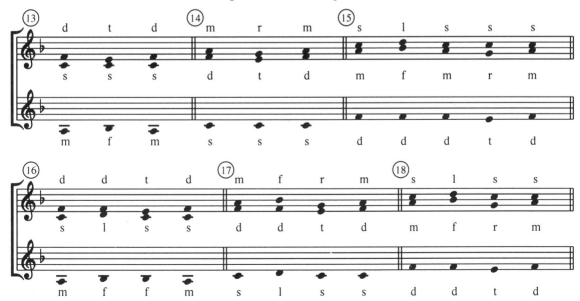

Full Scale Exercises In F

Review the new scale and pitch ladder, then sing these 2-line exercises separately or in any combination.

Lunch

When you come to a repeat sign, you go back to the beginning, or back to a sign in reverse. Look at the repeat signs in "Lunch." Where do the repeats go?

Repeat Sign

Brightly (♩ = 120)

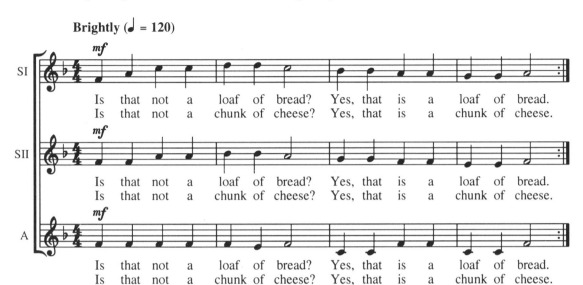

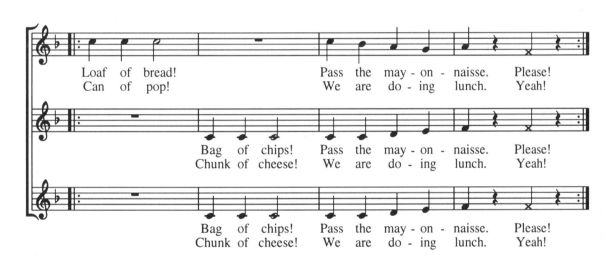

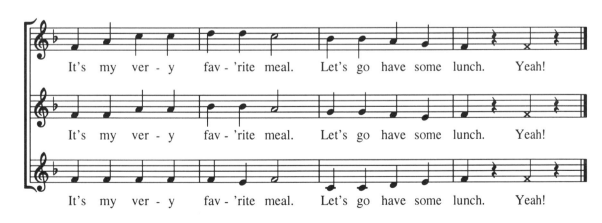

New Patterns
(Eighth Notes)

♩ = Ta

♫ = Ti – ti

Count each line.

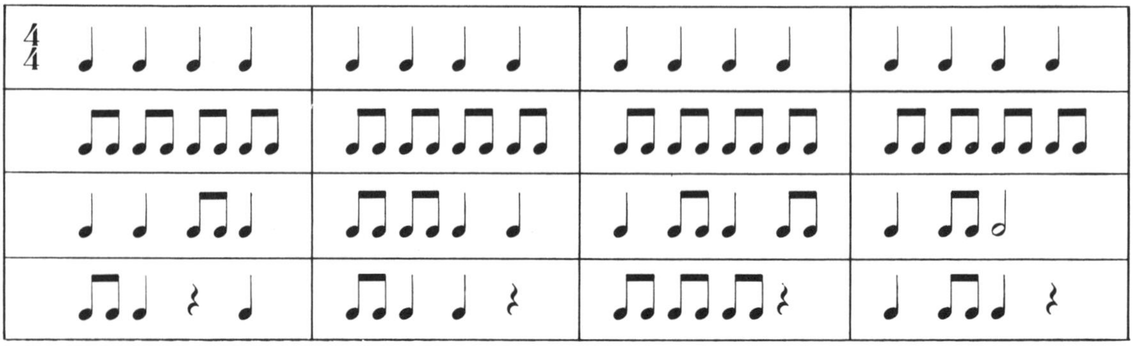

♫ may also be written as ♪♪ 
ti ti   ti ti

Eighth Notes And Rests In Action

Count the rhythm, find the starting pitch and go! Sing the lines separately and in any combination. In Exercise 8 you will notice an eighth rest (ɴ). Think "ti."

The Librarian

**Words and Music by
JOYCE EILERS and EMILY CROCKER**

New Patterns: $\frac{3}{4}$ and $\frac{2}{4}$

$\frac{3}{4}$ Practice

$\frac{2}{4}$ Practice

* In most music, a whole measure rest, even in $\frac{2}{4}$ and $\frac{3}{4}$, is written as ▬

Exercises in 3/4

Use the pitch ladder (tonic chord) to find the starting pitch. Sing separately and in any combination.

①

②

③

④

⑤

⑥

Exercises In 2/4

Use the pitch ladder (tonic chord) to find the starting pitch. Sing separately and in any combination.

(1)

(2)

(3)

(4)

(5)

(6)

Oh Dear, What Can The Matter Be

Traditional

Tie - see page 36

SIGHT–SINGING FOR SSA — Singer's Edition

Warm-ups And Tune-ups
(Key of C)

① Broken chords - practice until comfortable.

② All voices sing Exercise 2 until it seems easy, then interchange with Exercise 3.

③

Practice these chord drills, listening for balance, tuning and blend.

④ ⑤ ⑥

⑦ ⑧ ⑨

Ties

Ties in music are like addition signs in math. Just like the name says, they "tie" two notes

together. For counting purposes, if two 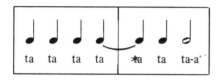 notes are tied , you just **drop the "t"**

from the second "ta" and it comes out . Ties often connect notes in different

measures.

reads: ta ta ta ta – a ta ta-a   reads: ta ta ta ta – a ta ta-a

This principle works with all sorts of notes.

Rhythm Practice

Practice With Tied Notes

Count the following lines. Be sure and drop the "t" sound when counting the ties. Then sing the lines in solfege separately and in any combination.

Mystery Melody

Sometimes a note is tied to a note on the next staff. Count and sing this song. Do you recognize the tune? Can you add the words?

* Take a quick advance look at page 40.

Slurs

Be careful not to confuse **ties** with **slurs.** Both look the same, but a **tie** connects two notes of the SAME pitch, while a **slur** connects two or more notes of a DIFFERENT pitch.

When you count music with slurs, you don't take the "t" sound off the second note.

Make New Friends

From "My Country 'Tis Of Thee"

This Special Day

Find the ties and slurs and count the rhythm before you sing this two-part song. Sing with pitch syllables, with a neutral syllable, such as "loo," and finally with words.

Ties And Slurs

Words and Music by
JOYCE EILERS and EMILY CROCKER

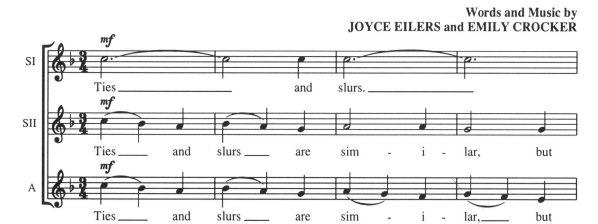

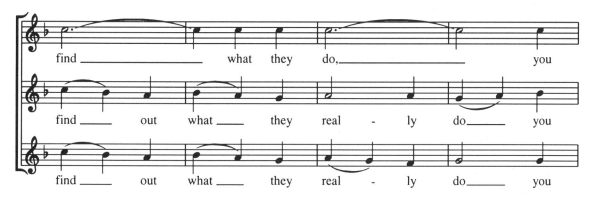

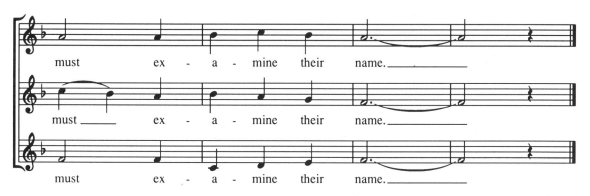

Dotted Notes

Sometimes tied notes are written in another way. For instance,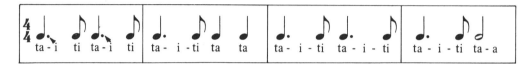

becomes  when the dot replaces the first "ti." The other note (♪) is

still a "ti" (refer to PATTERNS OF SOUND, VOL. I, p. 20).

By using dots, a song like this one . . .

My coun-try 'tis__ of thee, sweet land of li - ber-ty, of thee I sing.

can be written this way:

My coun-try 'tis of thee, sweet land of li - ber-ty, of thee I sing.

Practice

Count and sing these two–line exercises in any combination.

More Dotted Notes

Sometimes you find the reverse example ![♪ note | ti - ta-i], which is equal to ![note ti ti xa]

but since the dot is always placed **after** the note, we will say ![♪ note | ti - ta-i] for the sake

of uniformity. This sounds confusing till you try to use it!

Rhythm Practice

4/4 ♪♩. ♩ ♩	♪♩. ♩ ♩	♪♩. ♪♩.	♪♩. ♩
ti ta-i ta ta	ti ta-i ta ta	ti ta-i ti ta-i	ti ta-i ta - a
♩ ♩ ♪♩.	♩ ♪♩.	♪♩. ♩ ♩	♪♩. ♩
ta ta ti - ta-i	ta - a ti ta-i	ti ta-i ta ta	ti ta-i ta - a
♫♫♪♩.	♫♫♩	♫♫♪♩.	♪♩. ♩ ♩

On your own

Now you are ready for a two-line song that will fit with the three exercises on page 40. Sing it alone, and then in combination with the other three.

Dotted Note Practice

Use the pitch ladder to find your starting note, then sing these lines separately and in any combination.

Goodbye, Goodbye

**Words and Music by
JOYCE EILERS and EMILY CROCKER**

*Substitute names and places.

SIGHT–SINGING FOR SSA — Singer's Edition

Who Has Seen The Wind

Text by CHRISTINA ROSSETTI (Adapted)

**Music by JOYCE EILERS
and EMILY CROCKER**

46

D – Another New Key

On this page "do" again moves to a new place on the staff, and all the other notes move also. Drill until the examples seem easy.

The Scale

d r m f s l t d d r m r d d t l s f m r d d t l s l t d

Pitch Ladder (Tonic Chord)

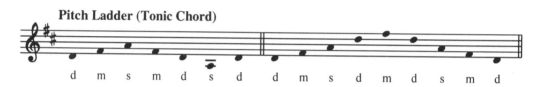

d m s m d s d d m s d m d s m d

Warm-ups And Tune-ups
(Key of D)

Practice these broken chords often, until the patterns become habit. Always listen to pitch, tuning the last note of the chord to the first note.

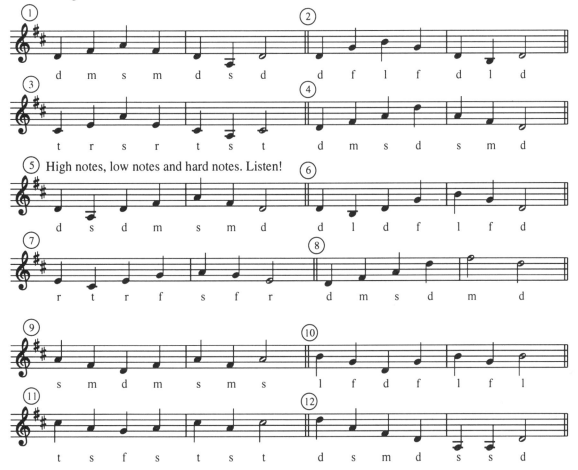

⑤ High notes, low notes and hard notes. Listen!

Chord Drills

Practice these chord drills, listening for balance, tuning and blend.

SIGHT–SINGING FOR SSA — Singer's Edition

Combinable Exercises in $\frac{4}{4}$

Sing each $\frac{4}{4}$ line separately and in any combination.

Combinable Exercises in $\frac{3}{4}$

Sing each $\frac{3}{4}$ line separately and in any combination. Don't rush!

As I Was Out Walking

Traditional Text

**Music by JOYCE EILERS
and EMILY CROCKER**

SIGHT–SINGING FOR SSA — Singer's Edition

How To Find "Do"

You can find "do" in any key if you memorize the following three simple rules.

Rule 1: If there are no sharps (♯) or flats (♭) after the clef sign (𝄞 or 𝄢),
"do" is automatically the key of C.

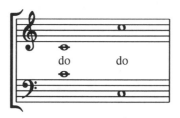

Rule 2: If there are flats after the clef sign (key signature), the flat farthest
to the right is "fa." Count up or down to "do."

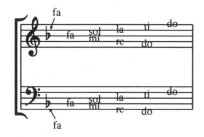
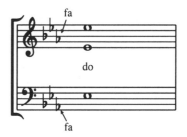

Rule 3: If there are sharps in the key signature, the sharp farthest to the right
is "ti." Count up or down to "do."

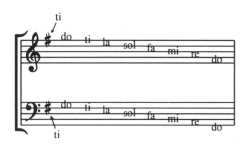
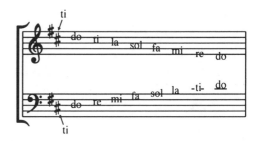

Key Change Practice

For each exercise, find "do," then sing a pitch ladder to establish the key and starting pitches.

More Key Change Practice

For each exercise, find "do," then sing a pitch ladder to establish the key.

Key of G

Practice the scale in both octaves ascending and descending.

d r m f s l t d   d t l s f m r d

② Sing the following pitch ladder patterns on your own, without the pitches written in.

Practice the following chord drills, listening carefully for balance, blend and tuning.

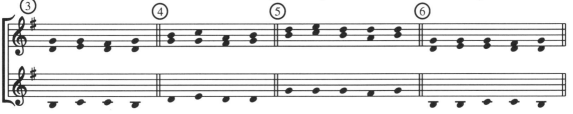

Good Luck Song

SI — See a pin and pick it up, all that day you'll have good luck.

SII — See a pin and pick it up, all that day you'll have good luck.

A — See a pin and pick it up, all that day you'll have good luck.

See a pin and let it lie, all that day you'll have to cry.

See a pin and let it lie, all that day you'll have to cry.

See a pin and let it lie, all that day you'll have to cry.

One I Love

Traditional Text

**Music by JOYCE EILERS
and EMILY CROCKER**

Syncopation Information

Combinable Exercises

Sing each line separately and in any combination.

Slovak Folk Song

Arranged with Original Lyrics by
JOYCE EILERS and EMILY CROCKER

TRADITIONAL

Key of B Flat

① Here is "do" in another new location. Drill until the examples are comfortable.

do re mi fa sol la ti do re mi fa sol

② ③ ④

do mi sol do sol mi do   do mi sol mi do sol do   do mi sol do mi sol mi do

Warm-ups and Tune-ups

⑤

⑥

Chord Drills

⑦ ⑧ ⑨ ⑩

⑪ ⑫ ⑬ ⑭

4/4 Exercises In B Flat

Sing each 4/4 exercise separately and in any combination.

3/4 Exercises In B Flat

Sing each 3/4 exercise separately and in any combination.

Maracas, Anyone?

Sing each exercise separately and in any combination. Can you make up words to go with each exercise?

New Patterns – Sixteenth Notes

♩ = ta

♫ = ti ti

♬♬ = ti ki ti ki

In Combinations

♬♬ may be written as ♪♪♪♪   Other combinations are possible: ♫♬ or ♬♫

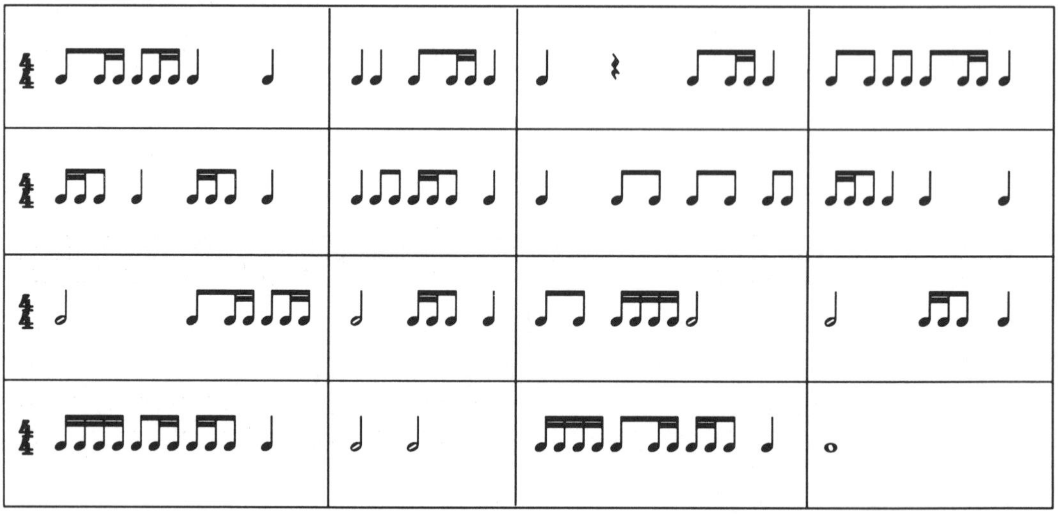

Not As Hard As It Looks

Review the key of C on page 35, then sing this page very slowly at first. It gets easier with practice. The exercises may be sung separately and in any combination.

Name That Tune

New Patterns ♩.♪

Review Ties and ♩. ♪

In many cases, a dot can replace a tie in a sixteenth note pattern as well, and the rhythm will be easier to read.

For example ♫♫ can be written ♩.♪
ti – i ki   ti ki

Be sure to think ♬♬ whenever you sing ♩.♪
ti ki ti ki   ti ki

Battle Hymn Of The Republic

**Arranged by JOYCE EILERS
and EMILY CROCKER**

TRADITIONAL

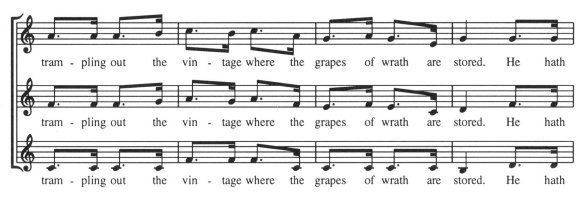

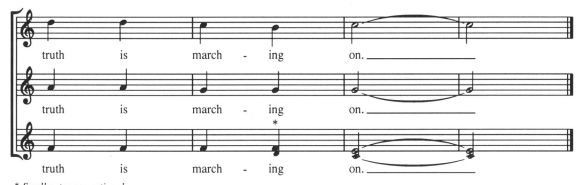

* *Small notes are optional.*

SIGHT–SINGING FOR SSA — Singer's Edition

Green Grow The Rushes

Traditional Text

**Music by JOYCE EILERS
and EMILY CROCKER**

Key Of E Flat

Drill until the examples are comfortable. Listen for balance, tuning and blend.

① The Scale ②

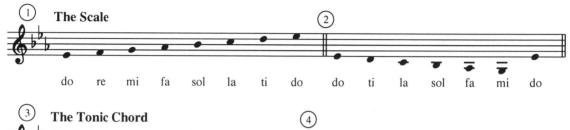

do   re   mi   fa   sol   la   ti   do   do   ti   la   sol   fa   mi   do

③ The Tonic Chord ④

do   mi   sol   do   sol   mi   do   do   sol   do   mi   sol   mi   do

Warm-ups And Tune-ups

Chord Drills

Mystery Tunes In E Flat

Can you identify these song fragments? Look over the rhythm, find "do" and sing the song in your mind.

Skater's Waltz

Arranged with Lyrics by
JOYCE EILERS and EMILY CROCKER

J. STRAUSS

Counting In Six – $\frac{6}{8}$

(Two Groups Of Three)

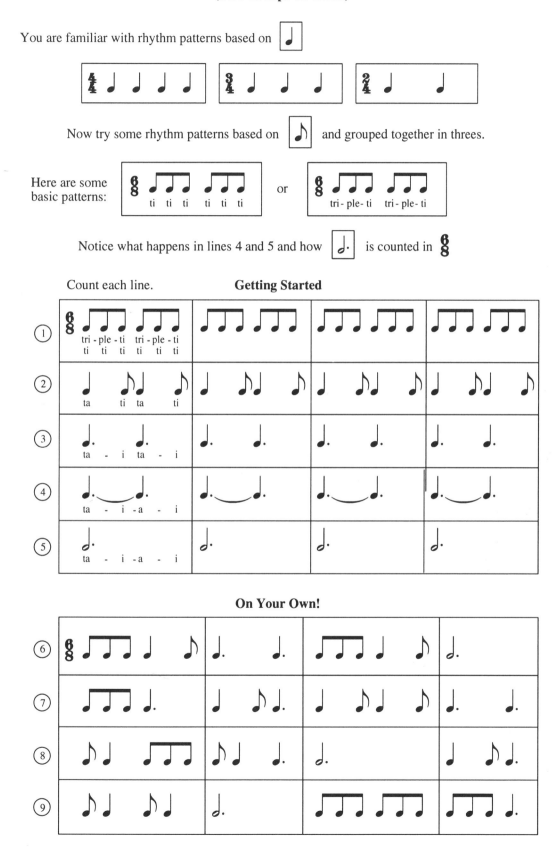

SIGHT–SINGING FOR SSA — Singer's Edition

$\frac{6}{8}$ Notes And Rests

♪ = ti		♪ = think ti	
♩♪ = ta–ti		‼♪ = think ta–ti	
♩· = ta–i		‼· = think ta–i	
♩· = ta–i–a–i		▬ = think ta–i–a–i	

On We Go — More $\frac{6}{8}$ Patterns

There are lots of possiblities for patterns. Try these new combinations of notes and rests and practice them until you are familiar with them as "patterns of sound."

New $\frac{6}{8}$ Combinations

Sing each of these two-line exercises separately and in combination with the others.

Name That Tune

Summer Is A–Coming In*

English (13th C.)

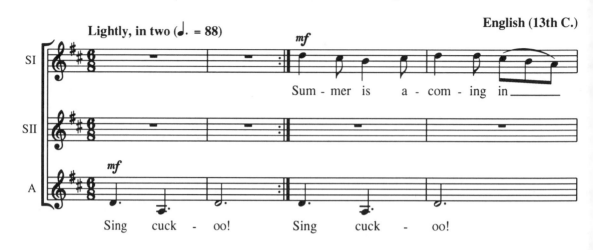

* This song dates back to the 13th century. While you may recognize
some of the words, many others have lost their meaning.

Accidentals

These three symbols are called accidentals and affect notes which follow them:

    1. A sharp (♯♩) raises a pitch by a half step.

    2. A flat (♭♩) lowers a pitch by a half step.

    3. A natural (♮♩) cancels a previous sharp or flat.

Here is a chart for determining the pitch syllable for an altered note:

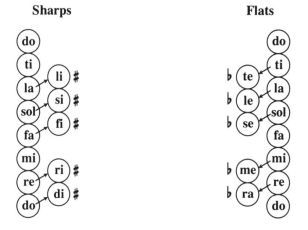

Sharps   **Flats**

Ascending Chromatic Scale

do   di   re   ri   mi   fa   fi   sol   si   la   li   ti   do

Descending Chromatic Scale

do   ti   te   la   le   sol   se   fa   mi   me   re   ra   do

Practice With Accidentals

If an accidental appears, it affects all following notes of the same pitch in the same measure, even though the accidental is stated only once.

do do di di do

do ti te te ti

If an accidental occurs in a tie over a barline, the accidental is not re-stated for the tied note, but should be re-stated for any following altered notes.

do re mi me me me me

Name That Tune

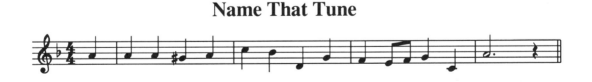

And This Tune

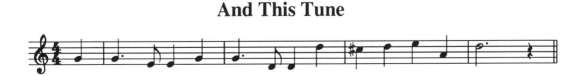

Fun With Accidentals

Notes that look different but sound the
same are called *enharmonic* notes.

Accidentals "Ain't" Easy

Don't rush *Find some enharmonic notes in the next song.*

On the key-board, you can see ac-ci-den-tals eas-i-ly.

On the key-board, you can see ac-ci-den-tals eas-i-ly.

On the key-board, you can see ac-ci-den-tals eas-i-ly.

When you sing it's an-oth-er thing! Ver-y hard to stay on key.

When you sing it's an-oth-er thing! Ver-y hard to stay on key.

When you sing it's an-oth-er thing! Ver-y hard to stay on key.

Chromatic Blues

A scale that moves by half-steps is called a "chromatic scale."
It is very difficult to sing, but give it a try!

Very Slow

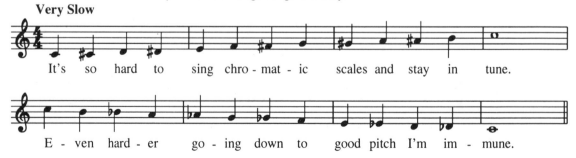

It's so hard to sing chro-mat-ic scales and stay in tune.

E-ven hard-er go-ing down to good pitch I'm im-mune.

Major And Minor

So far, all the songs and exercises in this book have been written in **major keys** in which the tonic chord is based on "do". There are many songs, however, which are based on "la" and are described as being in a **minor key**. Sing both examples and hear the differences between the two chords. In order to determine whether a song is in major or minor, look at the last note of the song. If the song ends with "do", "mi" and "sol" as the final chord, it is probably major; if it ends with "la", "do", "mi" as the final chord, then it probably is minor.

Major Chord

do   mi   sol   mi   do

Minor Chord

la   do   mi   do   la

Songs in minor often have accidentals, usually either the 6th or 7th notes of the scale. Try these three forms of the minor scale.

Natural Minor

la   ti   do   re   mi   fa   sol   la   sol   fa   mi   re   do   ti   la

Melodic Minor

la   ti   do   re   mi   fi   si   la   sol   fa   mi   re   do   ti   la

Harmonic Minor

la   ti   do   re   mi   fa   si   la   si   fa   mi   re   do   ti   la

SIGHT–SINGING FOR SSA — *Singer's Edition*

Major Keys And Their Relative Minor Keys

Major songs take their key name from "do." Since many songs are in a major key, you can usually check the location of "do" and know the name of the key. If the song title says "Sonata in F" they will mean F major, unless otherwise specified.

Minor songs take their key name from "la." As previously stated, they usually end on "la" and usually have several accidentals (especially on the 6th and 7th scale steps, making them "fi" and "si.")

Keys that share the same key signature (same amount of sharps or flats, etc.) are said to be "related." Therefore each major has a "relative minor key," and each minor key has a "relative major key." To find the name of the relative minor key, look for the letter name of "la." To find the name of the relative major key, look for the letter name of "do." Here are some examples of major keys and their relative minor keys,, with a tonic chord (pitch ladder) for each key.

Chord Drills

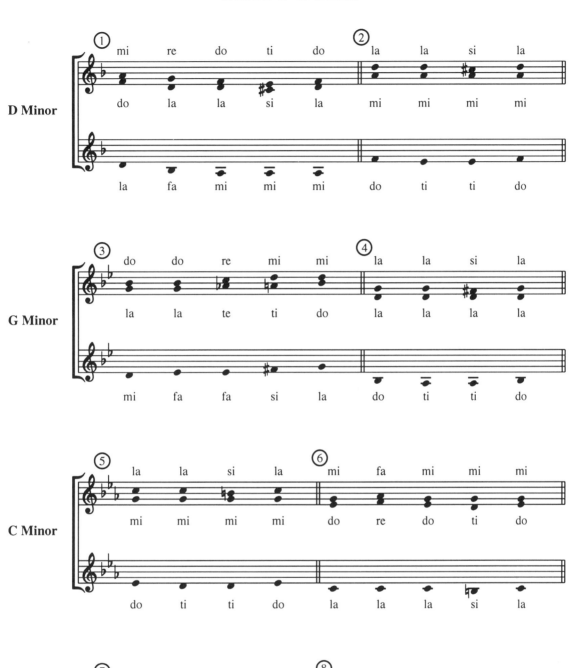

D Minor

G Minor

C Minor

F Minor

84

More Chord Drills

A Minor

E Minor

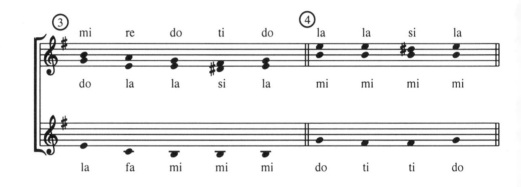

B Minor

F Sharp Minor

SIGHT–SINGING FOR SSA — Singer's Edition

Song Without Words

Modulation

Sometimes a song changes from one key to another. Usually there will be a new key signature when this happens, but occasionally the composer will use accidentals. When you are sight-reading in solfege, look ahead for these key changes and decide on a spot to "pivot" or switch into the new key. Look at this fragment of "When the Saints Go Marching In" and notice the pivot note.

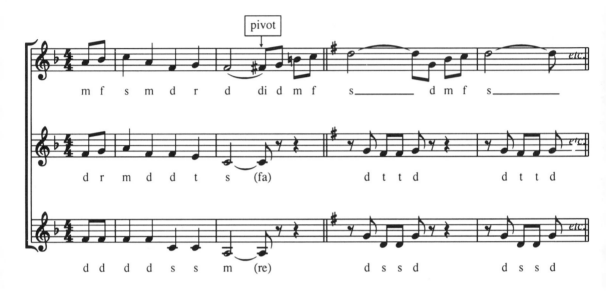

America The Beautiful

Try another fragment and see if you can determine the first key, the second key and the best spot to pivot.

Ev'ry Night When The Sun Goes In

Arranged by JOYCE EILERS
and EMILY CROCKER

TRADITIONAL

SIGHT–SINGING FOR SSA — Singer's Edition

88